IF ALL THE SEAS WERE ONE SEA

ETCHINGS BY JANINA DOMANSKA

MACMILLAN PUBLISHING CO., INC.
New York
COLLIER MACMILLAN PUBLISHERS
London

Macmillan Publishing Co., Inc.
866 Third Ave., New York, N.Y. 10022
Collier-Macmillan Canada Ltd.

Library of Congress catalog card number: 73-146621
Printed in the United States of America

3 4 5 6 7 8 9 10

The art was prepared in four colors—etchings on zinc plates for
blue and black and brush-and-ink overlays for red and green.
The typeface is Weiss roman, with display lettering etched by the artist.

TO SUSAN WITH LOVE

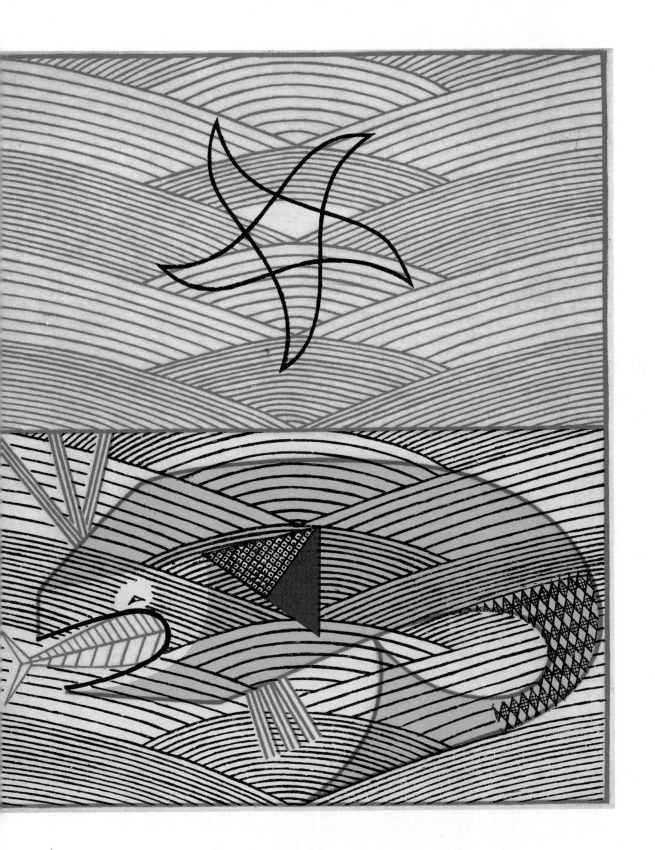

If all the seas were one sea,

what a great sea that would be.

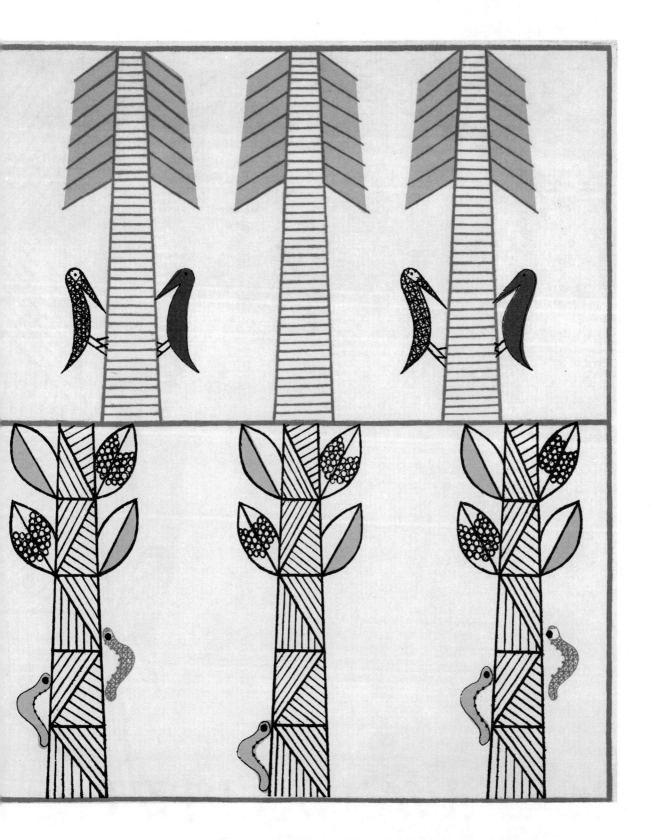

And if all the trees were one tree,

what a great tree that would be.

And if all the axes were one ax,

what a great ax that would be.

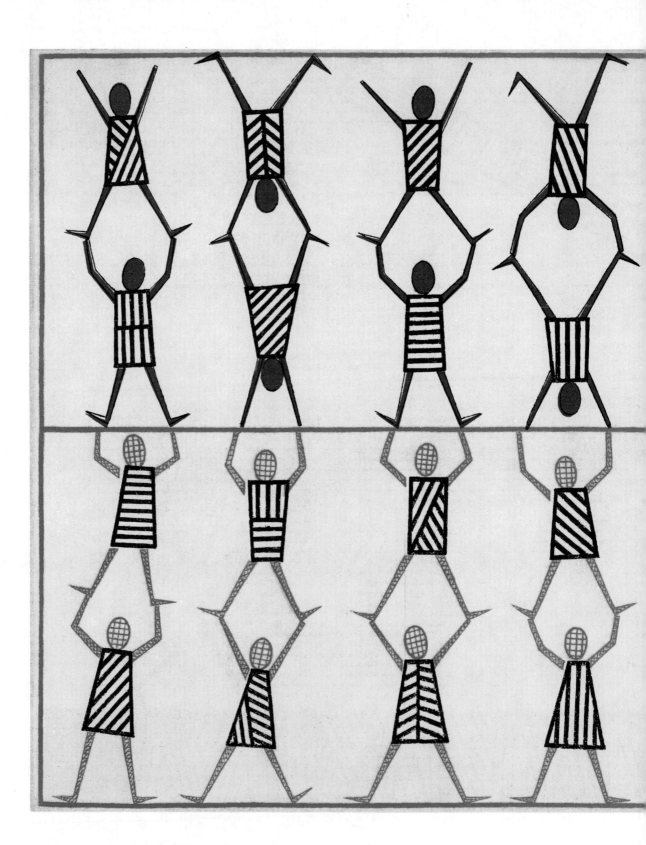

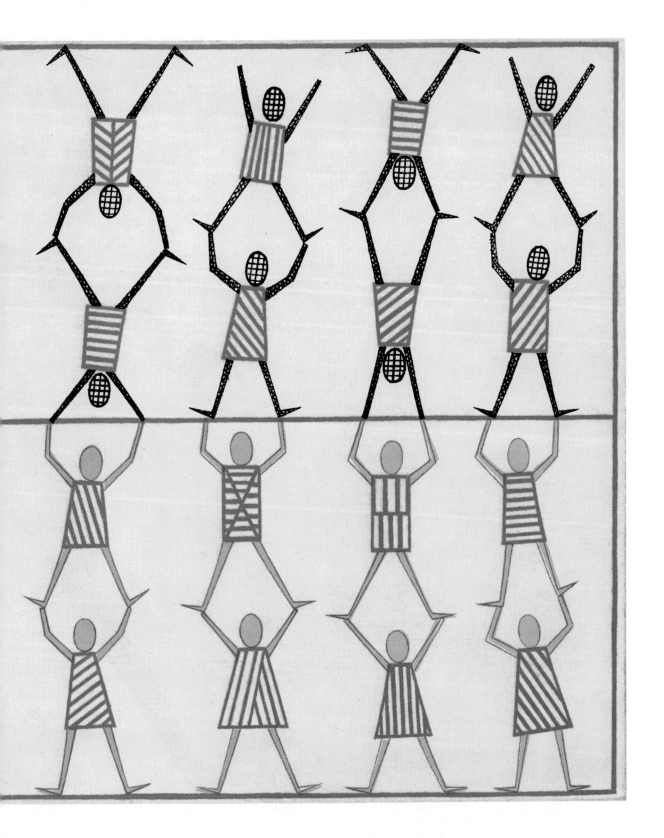

And if all the men were one man,

what a great man that would be.

And if the great man

took the great ax

and cut down the great tree

and let it fall

into the great sea,

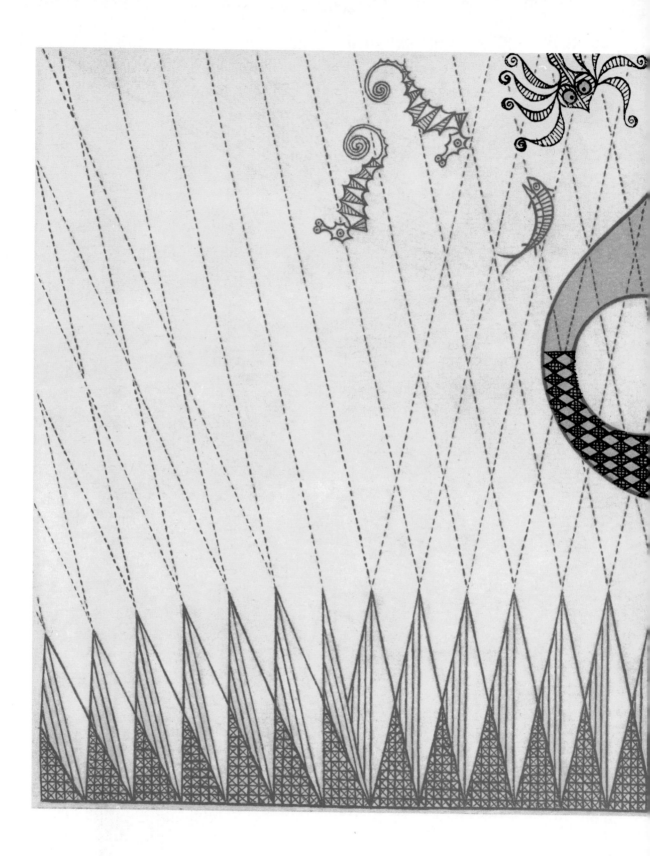

what a splish splash that would be!